To everyone who wanted to be a helicopter pilot but didn't.

Helicopter Pilots Are Better Than You 2.0

By Cassidy Krueger

With contributions by Kyle Krueger

Helicopter pilots are better than you because. . .

We make movies look cooler.

We helped take out Bin Laden.

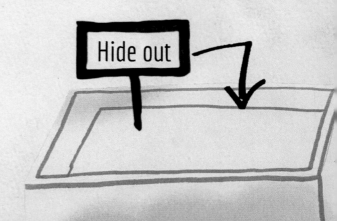

Hide out

We're special.

1/4 SM VISIBILITY

We're incredibly valuable.

Our fine motor skills transition better to the bedroom.

We can go places...

...You can't.

We're smarter and more skilled than you.

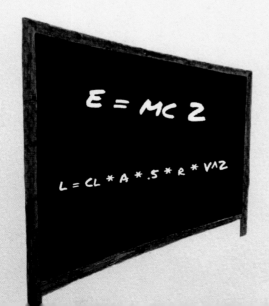

We save more lives.

Seriously,
We save
more
lives.

We can't help but look down on you.

We get it
up faster.

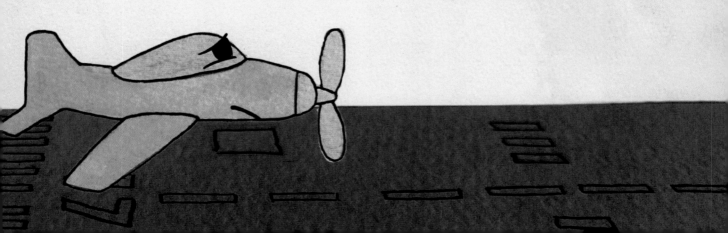

We're phenomenal conversation starters.

And we're extremely humble.

If this book offended you... you could
try not being such a little bitch.

Made in the USA
Monee, IL
11 February 2023

27522937R00024